Born to be Wild
Little Lions

Violette Rennert

Words that appear in the glossary are printed in
boldface type the first time they occur in the text.

GARETH**STEVENS**
GS
P U B L I S H I N G
A Member of the WRC Media Family of Companies

A Close Family

A little lion cuddles against the soft fur of its brothers and sisters, waiting for its mother to come back. She has gone hunting and has left them all alone. They are too young to see anything and do not yet know how to walk. When their mother returns, the baby lions, or cubs, eagerly drink her milk. When the cubs are finished

drinking, their mother looks over their hiding place. If a hyena, a leopard, or even an unfamiliar male lion found the cubs, it might kill them and eat them. To keep the cubs safe, their mother will take them to a new hiding place.

At birth, lion cubs are covered with spots that will disappear by the age of three months. Because of their spotted fur, cubs seem to disappear into the savanna grasses.

What do you think?

Who do lions live with?

a) They live alone.

b) They live with only a father and a mother.

c) They live in a group.

3

Lions live in a group called a pride.

When lion cubs are a little over one month old, their mother brings them to live in her pride. A pride is a big family that includes two to four male lions; several female lions, called lionesses; and many young lions. The lionesses in a pride are all related and are sisters, cousins, mothers, or grandmothers. Because the lionesses in a pride all have babies at the same time, their cubs have many cousins to play with and many mothers to comfort them. Young cubs are taken care of by both their mothers and their aunts.

When a pride needs food, all the lionesses hunt together, except one, who stays to watch over the cubs. If a cub is hungry, it will drink milk from the female watching over it, even if she is not its mother.

Although male lions can be fierce, they are usually gentle and patient when they play with the pride's cubs.

A lion pride can have up to thirty animals. When a pride becomes very large, it will sometimes split into two groups. Both groups will continue to get along together.

It's Playtime!

When a little lion is about two months old, it is big enough to **venture** into the wild. Along with the other cubs in the pride, it follows the lionesses when they go hunting. Hidden in the tall grass, the cubs watch everything. **Gnus** and zebras quietly eat the grasses. The lionesses hug the ground before jumping up to attack them. What a show! Before the cubs learn how to hunt for themselves, they spend hours playing — pretending to hunt. One cub pretends to be the **prey**, another pretends to be the hunter.

What do you think?

How often do lions eat?

a) three times a day

b) once a day

c) three times a week

A lion cub starts catching small prey at about nine months old. At about ten months of age, a cub stops drinking its mother's milk and then eats only meat.

Lions eat about three times a week.

Lions are **carnivores**. They eat almost nothing but meat. A lion can eat up to 50 pounds (23 kilograms) of meat at one time! After eating, a lion rests for several days to digest its food. Lions hunt large **herbivores**, such as zebras, antelopes, and gnus. During the dry season, lions will wait for their prey near bodies of water, where these animals come to drink.

A lion uses its powerful jaws and very sharp teeth to attack and kill its prey. The lion eats almost all parts of the animals it catches.

Hunting is the job of the pride's lionesses. They can hide from prey more easily than male lions, because the females do not have manes. The females are also smaller, faster, and more clever than the males.

Lionesses hunt as a group at nightfall or at dawn. To catch animals that are bigger and faster than themselves, they must work together and surprise their prey.

Male lions rarely join in the hunt, but they always eat first. Then the lionesses eat. The cubs eat last. If there is no food left, the cubs have to wait until the next hunt to eat.

Sleeping, Sleeping, and More Sleeping

There are many ways for a little lion to take a nap: lying against its mother, tucked between its father's legs, curled up in the shade of an **acacia**, perched on top of a tree, stretched out on its back or on its stomach. A little lion never gets tired of sleeping because sleeping is one of its most important activities. Even adult lions sleep about twenty hours a day. They are awake only about four hours to hunt, eat, and play with their cubs.

To call her cubs, a lioness meows like a cat. The cubs quickly respond. When a lioness is angry, she gives a low growl or growls and shows her teeth.

What do you think?

Why do lions roar?

a) to show they are happy

b) to communicate with each other

c) to scare their prey

Lions roar to communicate with each other.

Roaring helps lions in the pride stay in contact with each other, especially when they become separated, such as during a hunt. Grrrr! Grrrr! Sometimes, all the lions in a pride will roar together, maybe a dozen times, louder and louder before gradually stopping. When they hear an unfamiliar lion passing by, they roar to tell it to leave their **territory** right away. Even from as far away as 3 miles (5 kilometers), when another animal hears the roars, it will leave the area.

To tell one lion from another, humans look at the rows of black spots above lions' mouths. These "whisker spots" form patterns that are different on each lion.

Lions love to sleep in trees, where they are sheltered from the Sun's heat and from biting horseflies.

Lions can sleep out in the open during the middle of the day because they know that no animal will risk coming near them. Adult lions do not have any enemies except humans.

Like pet cats, lions have **retractable** claws. They can move their claws in and out as often as they need to. Lions use their sharp claws to catch prey, climb trees, and scratch the ground.

Leaving the Pride

When a male lion is about three years old, it is almost an adult. Its mane has grown a lot, it knows how to hunt, and it must now leave the pride. With one or two of its brothers or cousins, it will form a small group of young males. Together, they will wander the plains and the savanna hunting. When they become very strong, they will try to find a place in another pride. They will challenge the oldest males in a pride, and the strongest of the young lions will become that pride's new leader.

What do you think?

Why does a male lion have a mane?

a) to scare other animals

b) to show it is the king

c) to help keep it warm

At about five months of age, a tuft of black hair will start developing at the tip of a lion cub's tail. A male lion's mane will not start growing until he is two years old. By the time he is five years old, the mane will be long and thick.

A male lion has a mane to scare other animals.

Lionesses hunt and take care of the cubs, while male lions protect the pride's territory. The territory is the area where the pride lives. The size of a pride's territory depends on the amount of prey that can be found there. The more food lions can find to eat, the smaller their territory needs to be. Lions in a pride do not want lions they do not live with in their territory. The males in a pride growl to scare other lions away. If unknown lions still enter, then the males must fight the intruders to chase them away. The pride's males must be very strong because if they lose the fight, the other lions will take over their positions in the pride.

With its large mane, a male lion is so impressive and scary that other animals avoid disturbing it. When the male has to fight, its mane protects it against bites and scratches.

Life is easy for males in a pride, but the easy life lasts only two to ten years. As soon as they become weak, male lions are pushed out of their prides by younger, stronger males and must live by themselves.

To help protect their prides, lions mark their territories by scratching the ground and trees and leaving their scents on bushes. These signs let other animals know they are in a pride's territory.

Friends for Life

A young lioness spends her entire life in the pride with her mother, aunts, sisters, and female cousins. When she is about three years old, she reaches her adult size and is ready to have cubs of her own. One day, she goes away with one of the pride's male lions. The pair

will **mate** several times over the next few days before returning to the pride. Three and a half months later, the young lioness will go off by herself and give birth to her cubs.

Lionesses have three to five cubs in each **litter**. The cubs each weigh a little over 2 pounds (1 kg), about the size of a two-month-old pet kitten. Newborn lion cubs are fully dependent on their mothers.

What do you think?

How does a lioness carry her cubs from place to place?

a) with her mouth

b) in her arms

c) on her back

A lioness carries her cubs with her mouth.

A lioness has a litter of cubs every two years. Females in the same pride usually give birth at the same time. The mothers gather when the cubs are one month old and look after all the little lions together. The male lions are often absent, but they help take care of the cubs when they are around. The males play with the little cubs and do not get upset when the cubs nibble on their tails or manes. Sometimes, however, the lions must tell them enough is enough!

When a lioness moves her babies or brings them to the pride, she carefully picks them up by the backs of their necks and carries them with her mouth.

Lion cubs drink their mother's milk for about three months before starting to eat meat.

A male lion is usually loving and gentle with cubs, but when a lion takes over a pride, it sometimes kills the cubs. It does not want to raise another lion's cubs and quickly mates with the lionesses to have cubs of his own.

Lions are **mammals**. They live mainly in protected areas in Africa, although a small number of lions are found in Asia. Lions live about thirteen years in the wild and up to thirty years in captivity. An adult male lion weighs between 350 and 550 pounds (159 and 250 kg). A female weighs between 250 and 300 pounds (113 and 136 kg).

Lions are **felines** and are related to all other cats, including tigers, leopards, cheetahs, and even pet cats!

A lion has dark bands on the backs of its rounded ears. Lions have very good hearing.

From its nose to the beginning of its tail, a male lion can measure up to about 10 feet (3 meters) long. A lioness is about 12 inches (30 centimeters) shorter.

A lion's mane can be blond, black, or red. As the lion grows older, its mane becomes darker.

From the ground to its shoulders, a lion can reach a height of about 46 inches (117 cm).

A lion has round, yellow eyes and can see well in dim light.

With their powerful legs, lions can run at speeds of up to 35 miles (55 km) an hour — faster than a car on a city street — but only for short distances.

23

GLOSSARY

acacia — a small tree with feathery leaves and white or yellow flowers

carnivores — animals that eat the meat of other animals

felines — members of the cat family, which includes lions, tigers, leopards, and pet cats

gnus — large African antelopes with short manes, long tails, and curved horns

herbivores — mammals that eat only plants

litter — a group of young animals born at the same time to the same mother

mammals — warm-blooded animals that have backbones, give birth to live babies, feed their young with milk from the mother's body, and have skin that is usually covered with hair or fur

mate — (v) join together to produce young

prey — (n) animals that are hunted and killed by other animals, usually for food

retractable — able to be pulled back or pulled inside, such as a cat's claws

savanna — a large, flat area of grassland with scattered trees, found in warm parts of the world

territory — an area of land that animals occupy and defend

venture — to take on the risks and dangers of an activity

Please visit our web site at: www.garethstevens.com
For a free color catalog describing Gareth Stevens Publishing's list of high-quality books and multimedia programs, call 1-800-542-2595 (USA) or 1-800-387-3178 (Canada). Gareth Stevens Publishing's fax: (414) 332-3567.

Library of Congress Cataloging-in-Publication Data

Rennert, Violette.
 [Petit lion. English]
 Little lions / Violette Rennert. — North American ed.
  p. cm. — (Born to be wild)
 ISBN 0-8368-4737-7 (lib. bdg.)
 1. Lions—Infancy—Juvenile literature. I. Title. II. Series.
QL737.C23R45513 2005
599.757'139—dc22   2004065368

This North American edition first published in 2006 by
Gareth Stevens Publishing
A Member of the WRC Media Family of Companies
330 West Olive Street, Suite 100
Milwaukee, Wisconsin 53212 USA

This U.S. edition copyright © 2006 by Gareth Stevens, Inc.
Original edition copyright © 2002 by Mango Jeunesse.

First published in 2002 as *Le petit lion* by Mango Jeunesse, an imprint of Editions Mango, Paris, France.

Picture Credits (t = top, b = bottom, l = left, r = right)
Bios: N. Granier cover, 20(tr); M. and C. Denis-Huot 7, 9(t), 20(b); B. Mikaelsen/P. Arno 13(tl); M. Nicolotti 13(bl), 21; R. Puillandre 12. Colibri: A. M. Loubsens title page, 5(both), 6, 14, 16, 22–23; D. Haution 8(b), 17(b); A. Saunier 13(r); C. Ratier 18. Phone: J. Sierra 8(t); M. Grenet/Soumillar 9(b); Labat/Ferrero 15; J.M. Labat 17(t), 22, back cover. Sunset: Horizon Vision 2, 4, 10, 19; G. Lacz 3, 11.

English translation: Muriel Castille
Gareth Stevens editor: Barbara Kiely Miller
Gareth Stevens art direction: Tammy West
Gareth Stevens designer: Jenni Gaylord

Printed in the United States of America

1 2 3 4 5 6 7 8 9 09 08 07 06 05